If I were asked to define
– Motherhood –
I would have defined it as love in its purest form.
– Unconditional Love –

~ Revathi Sankaran

Be•Inspired
A subsidiary of:
Two Girls and a Reading Corner
© 2021 Mandy Leigh
ISBN: 978-1-952879-39-5

Two Girls and a Reading Corner
PO Box 2404, Madison, Al 35758

www.twogirlsandareadingcorner.com

"To all mothers in every circumstance, including those who struggle, I say, 'Be peaceful. Believe in God and yourself. You are doing better than you think you are.'" — Jeffrey R. Holland

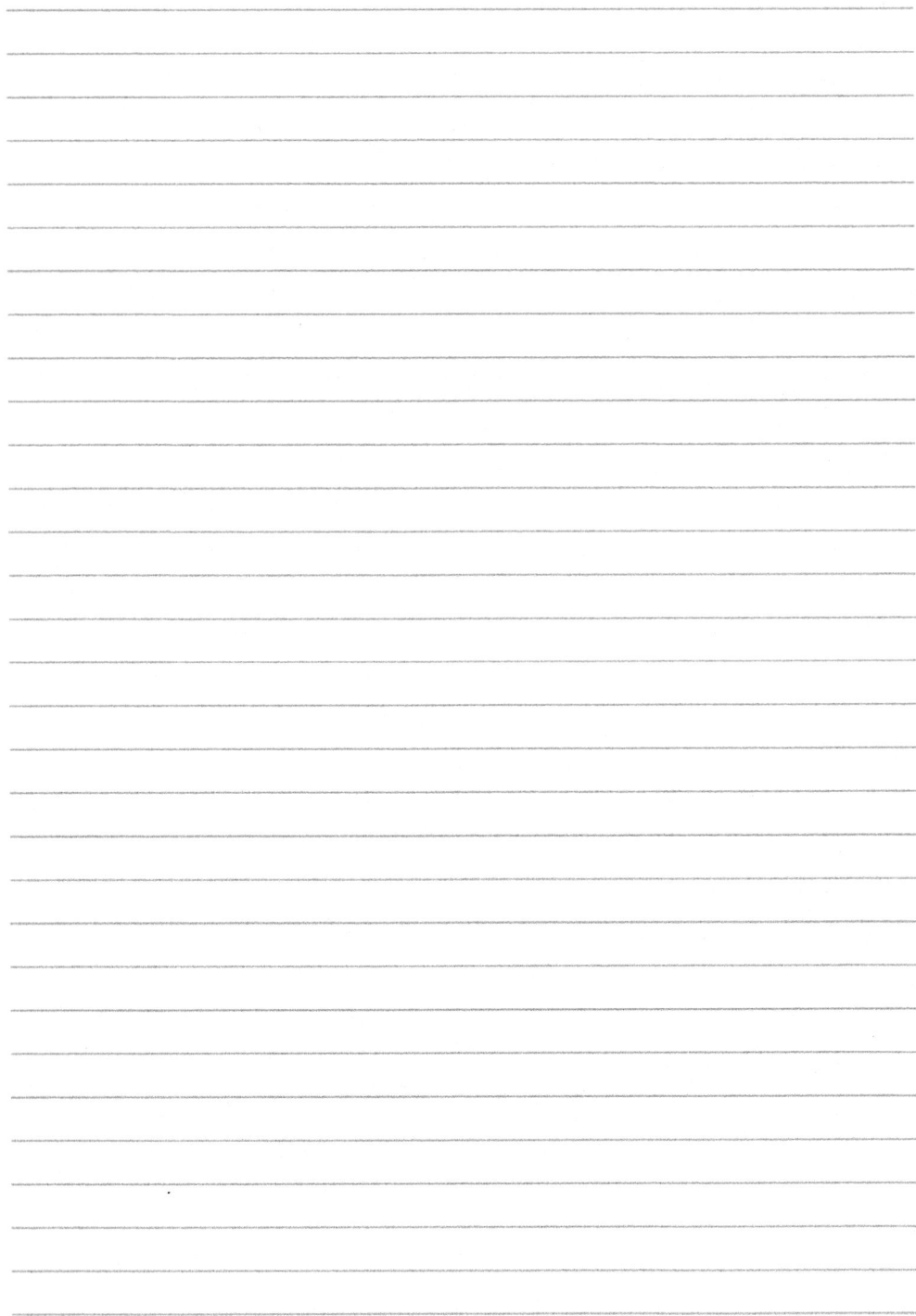

"Mother is a verb. It's something you do. Not just who you are."
– Dorothy Canfield Fisher

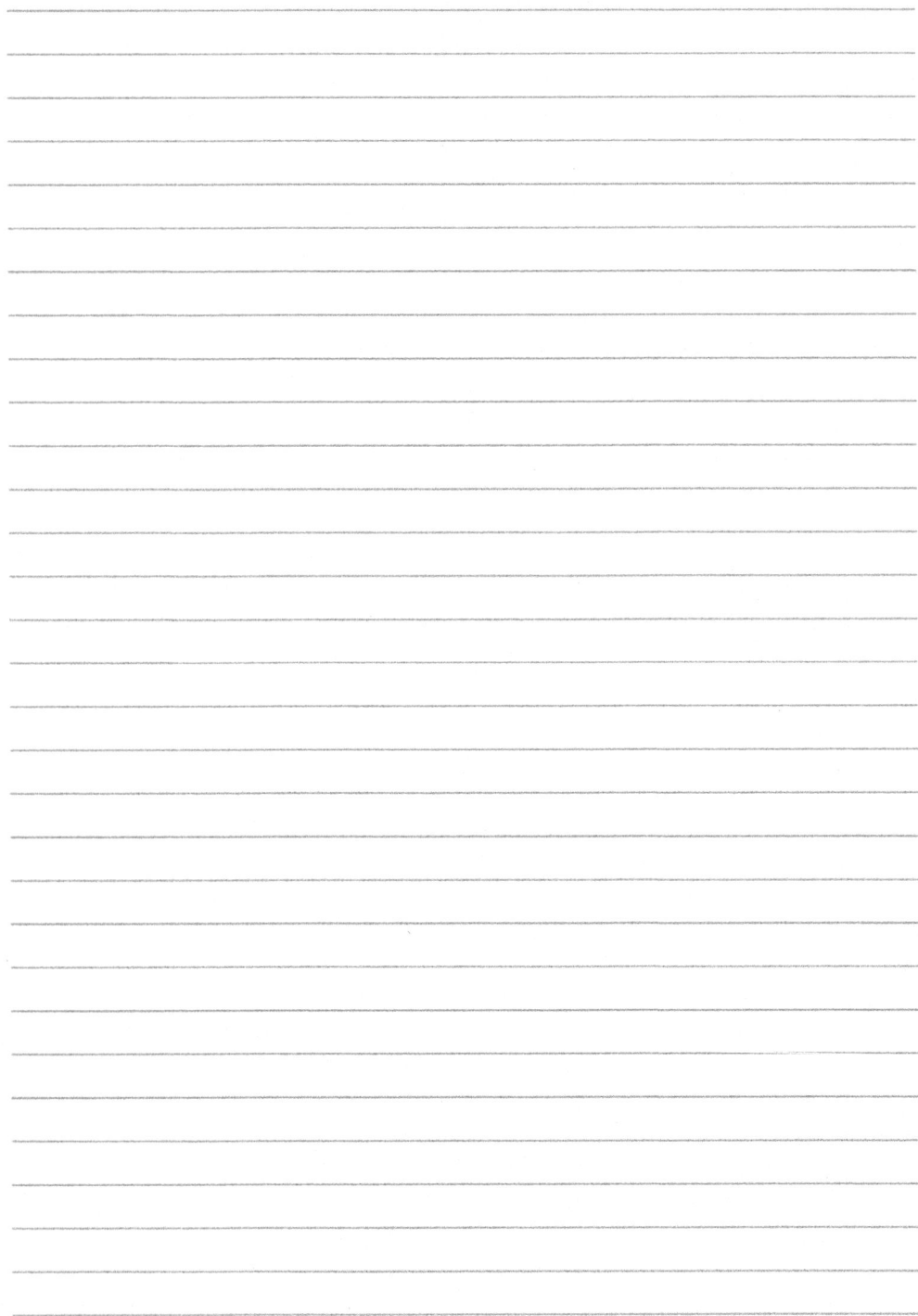

"There is nothing as powerful as mother's love, and nothing as healing as a child's soul." – Unknown

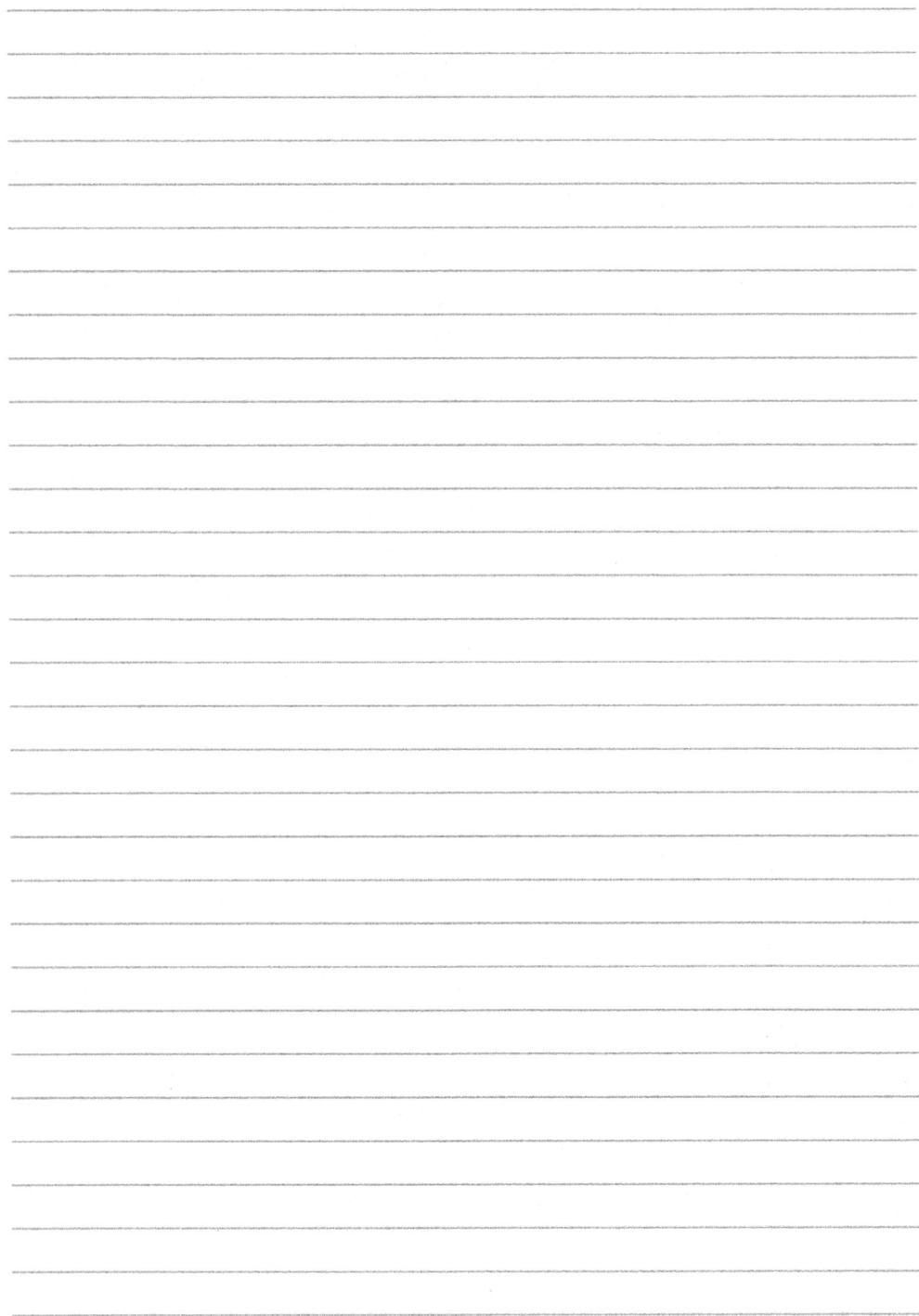

"I loved you before I knew you." – Unknown

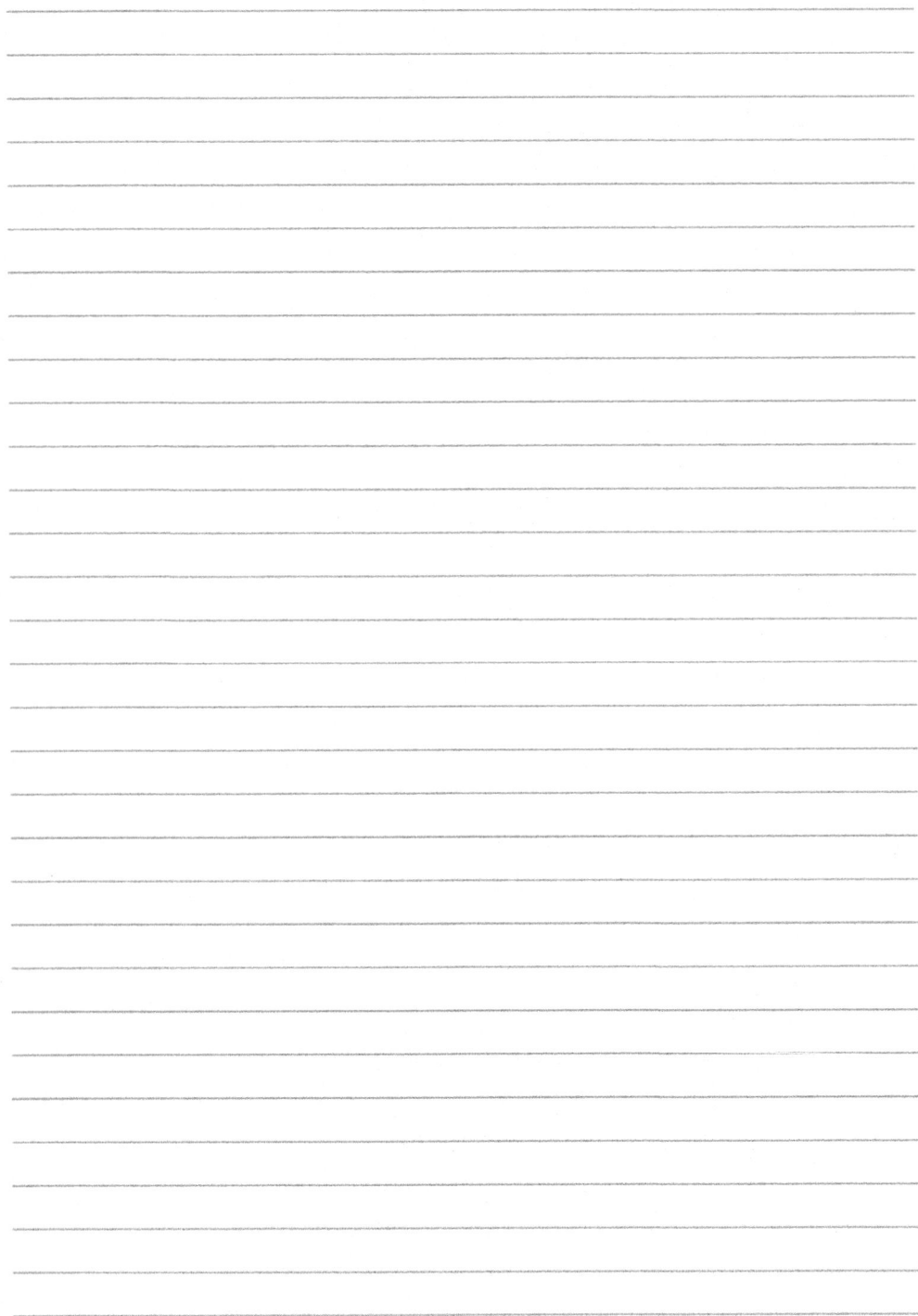

"A mother's love endures through all."– Washington Irving

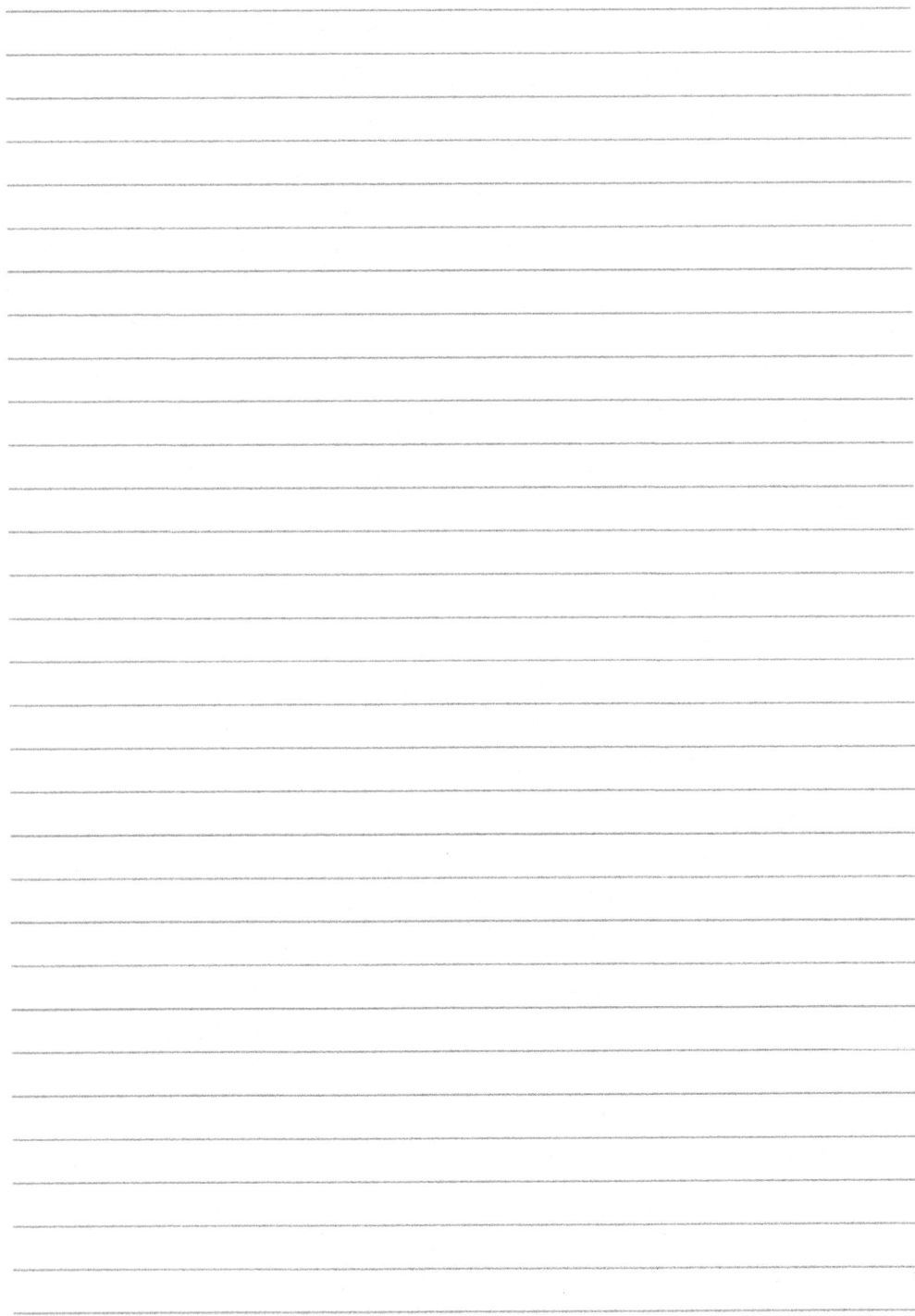

And now these three remain: faith, hope and love. But the greatest of these is love. - 1 Corinthians 13:13

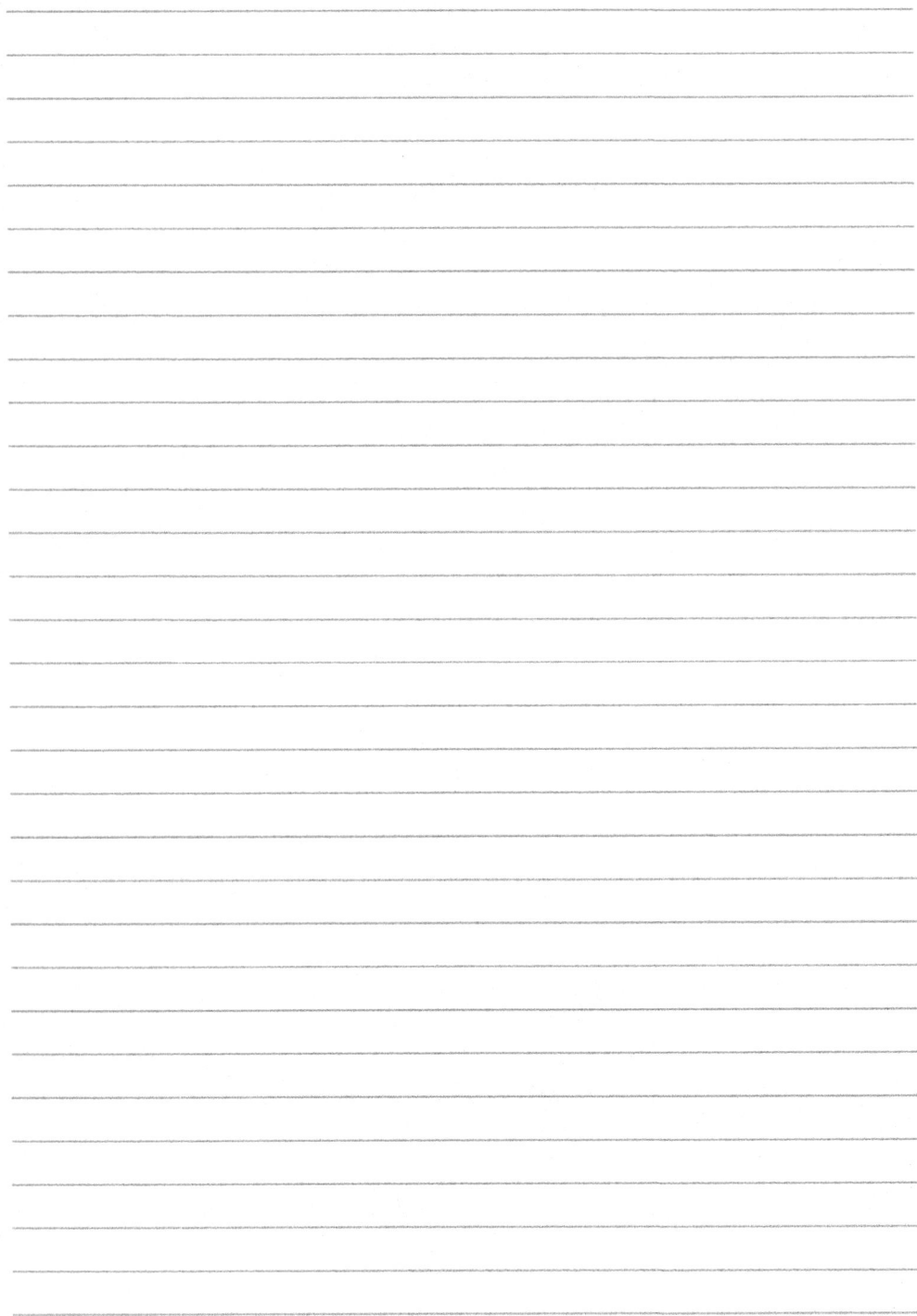

"Motherhood: All love begins and ends there." – Robert Browning

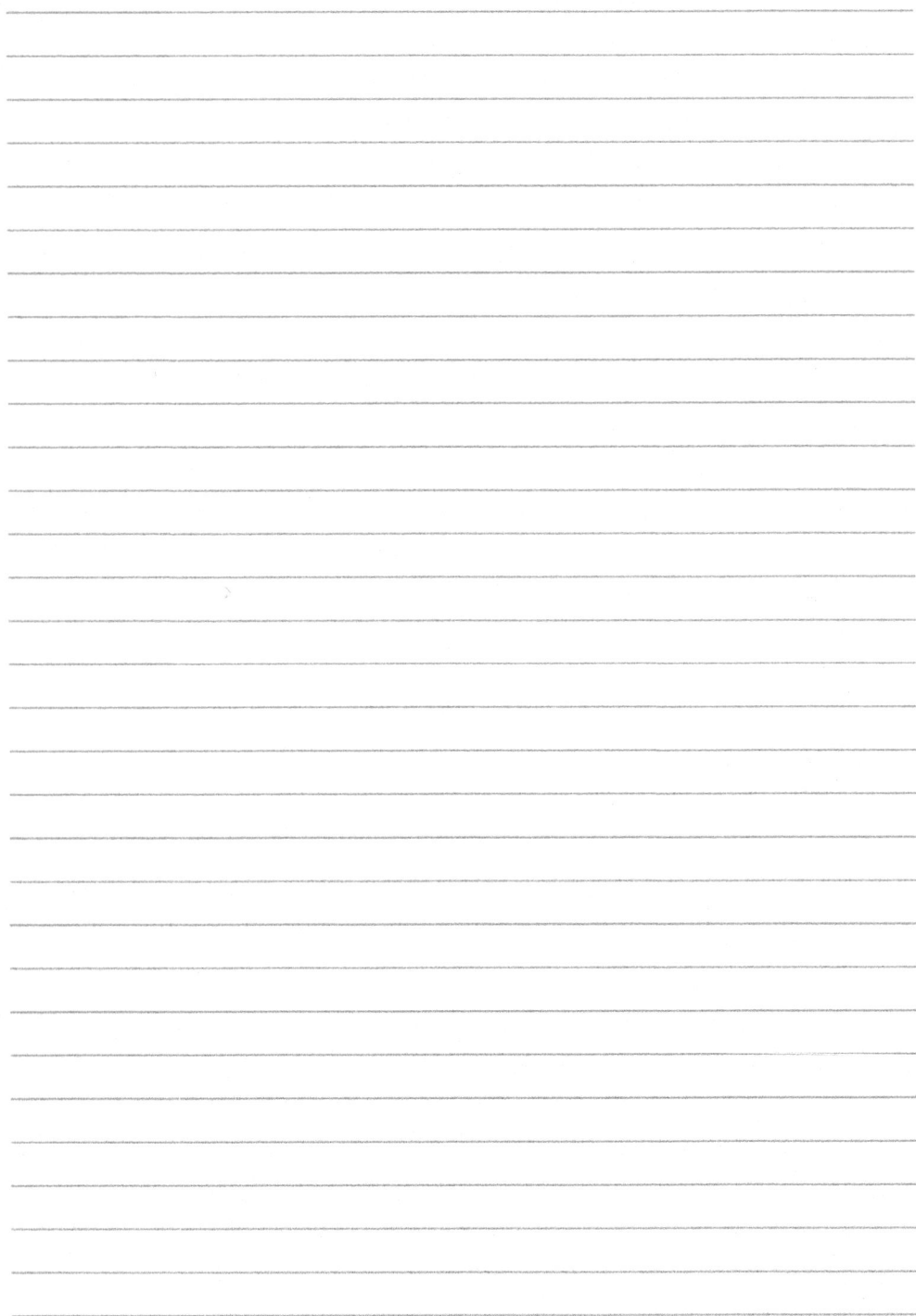

"There is no perfect way to be a mother and a million ways to
be a good one." -Jill Churchill

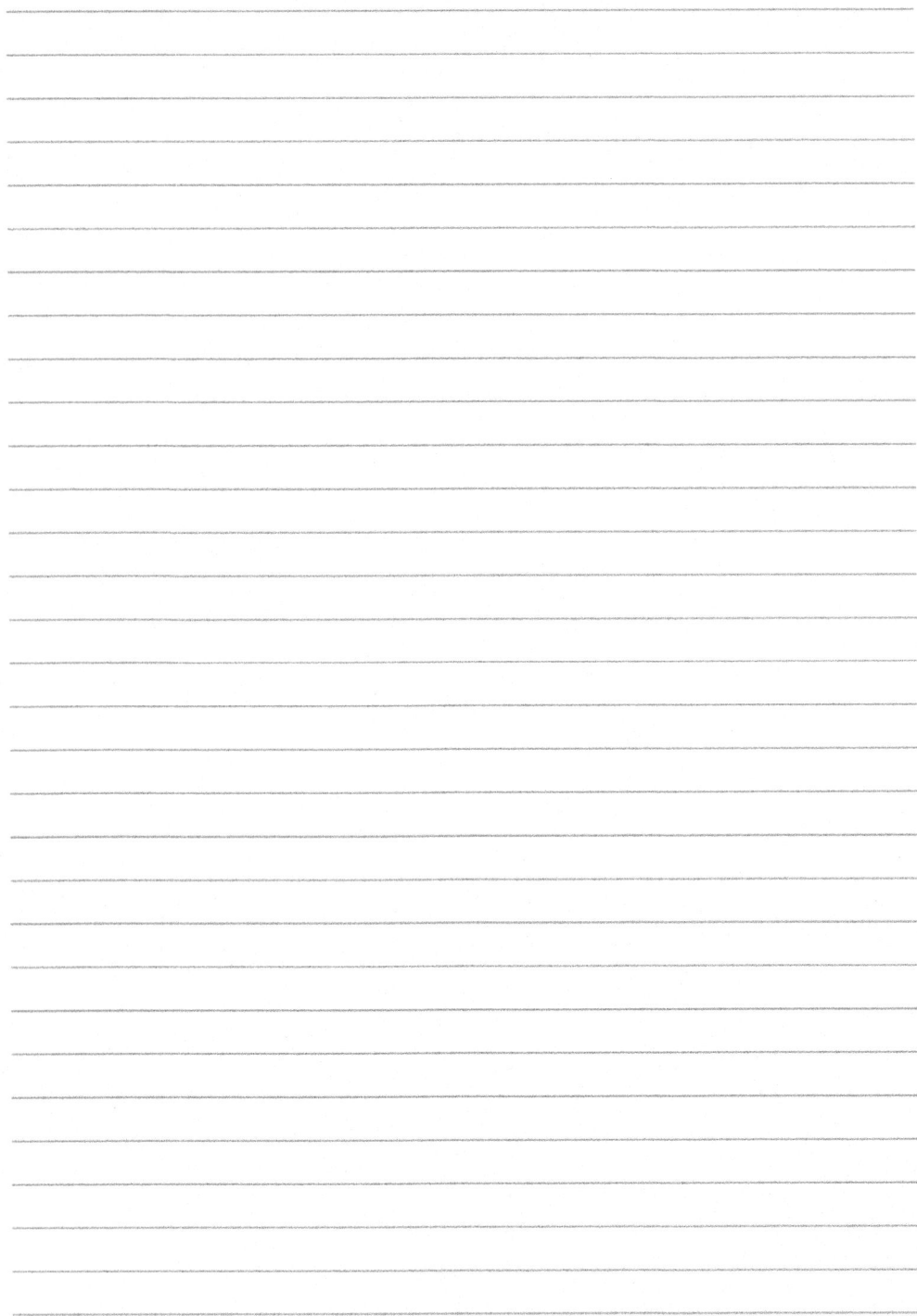

"Motherhood is a delicate balance between holding on and letting go."
-Unknown

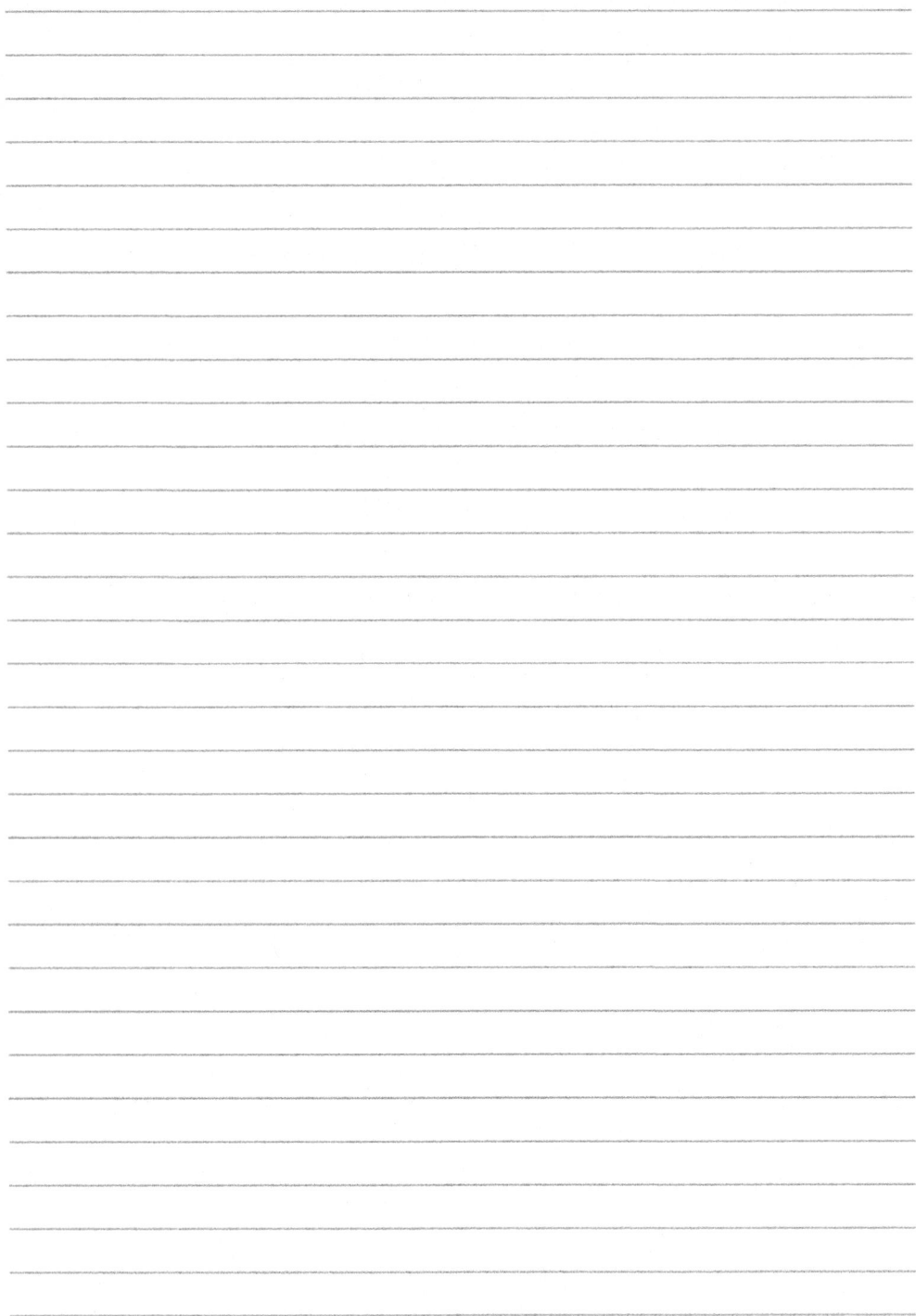

"Motherhood: the days are long, but the years are short."
-Gretchen Rubin

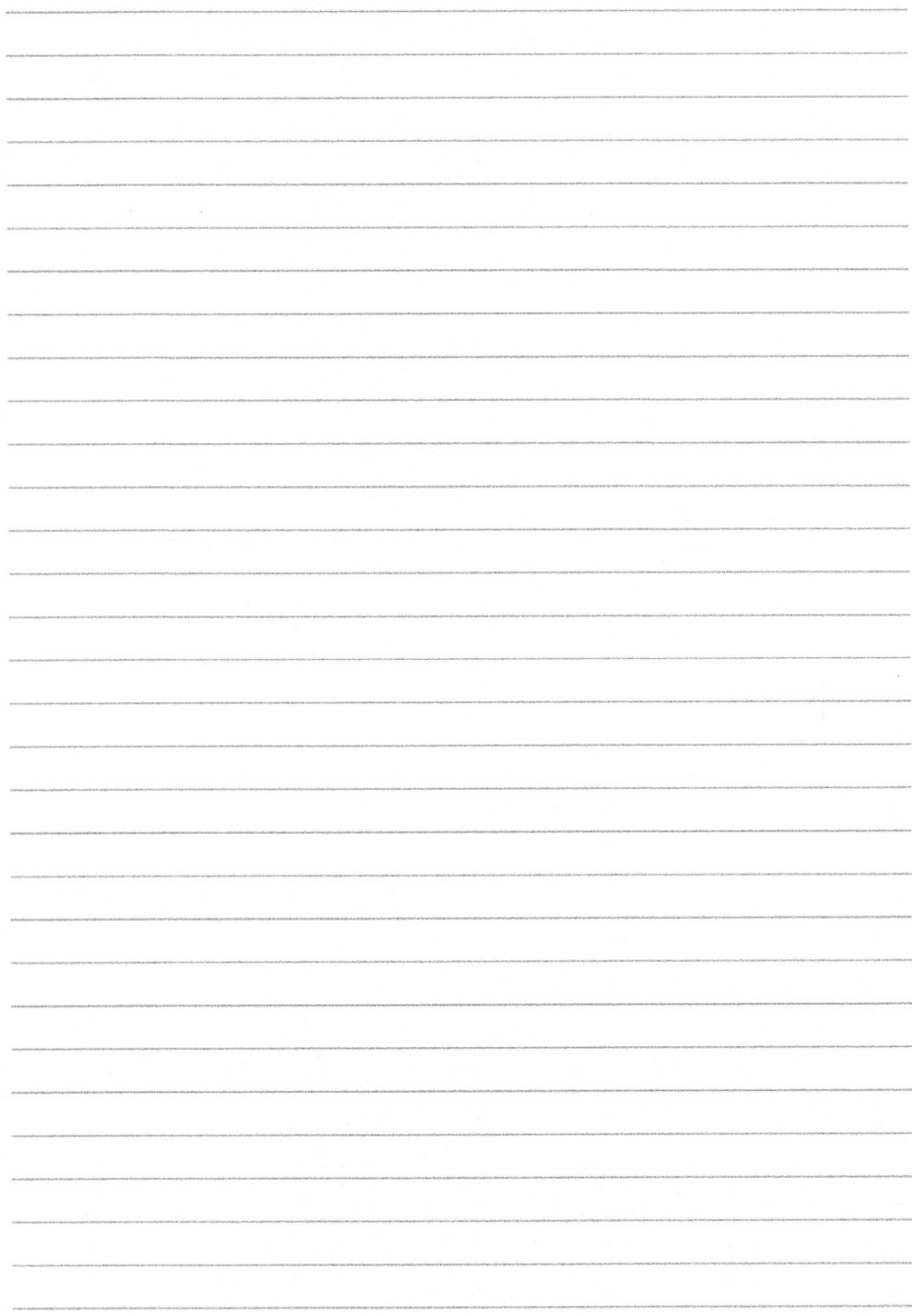

"There is no such thing as a perfect parent. So just be a real one."
-Sue Atkins

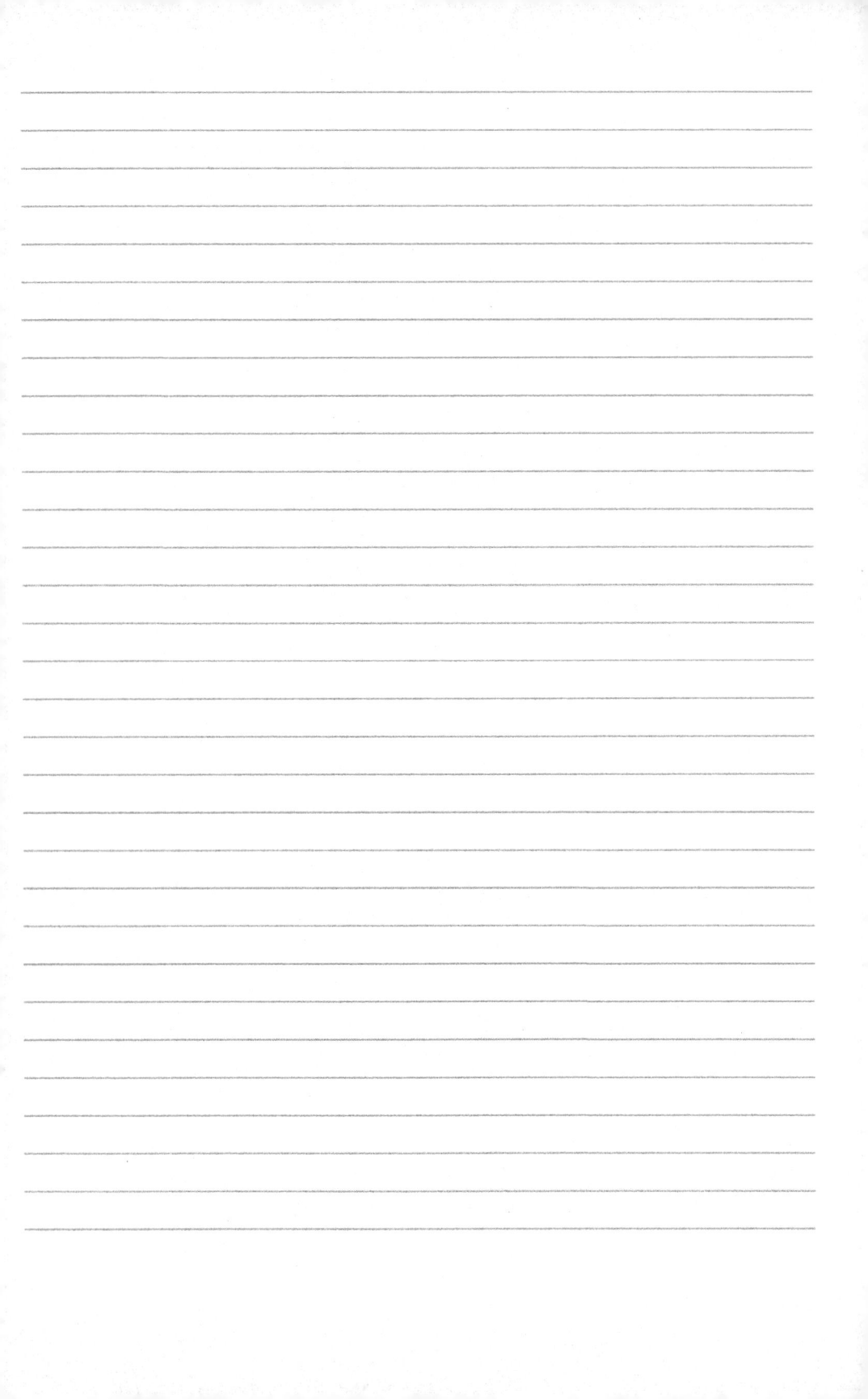

"To the world you are a mother, but to your family you are the world."
-Unknown

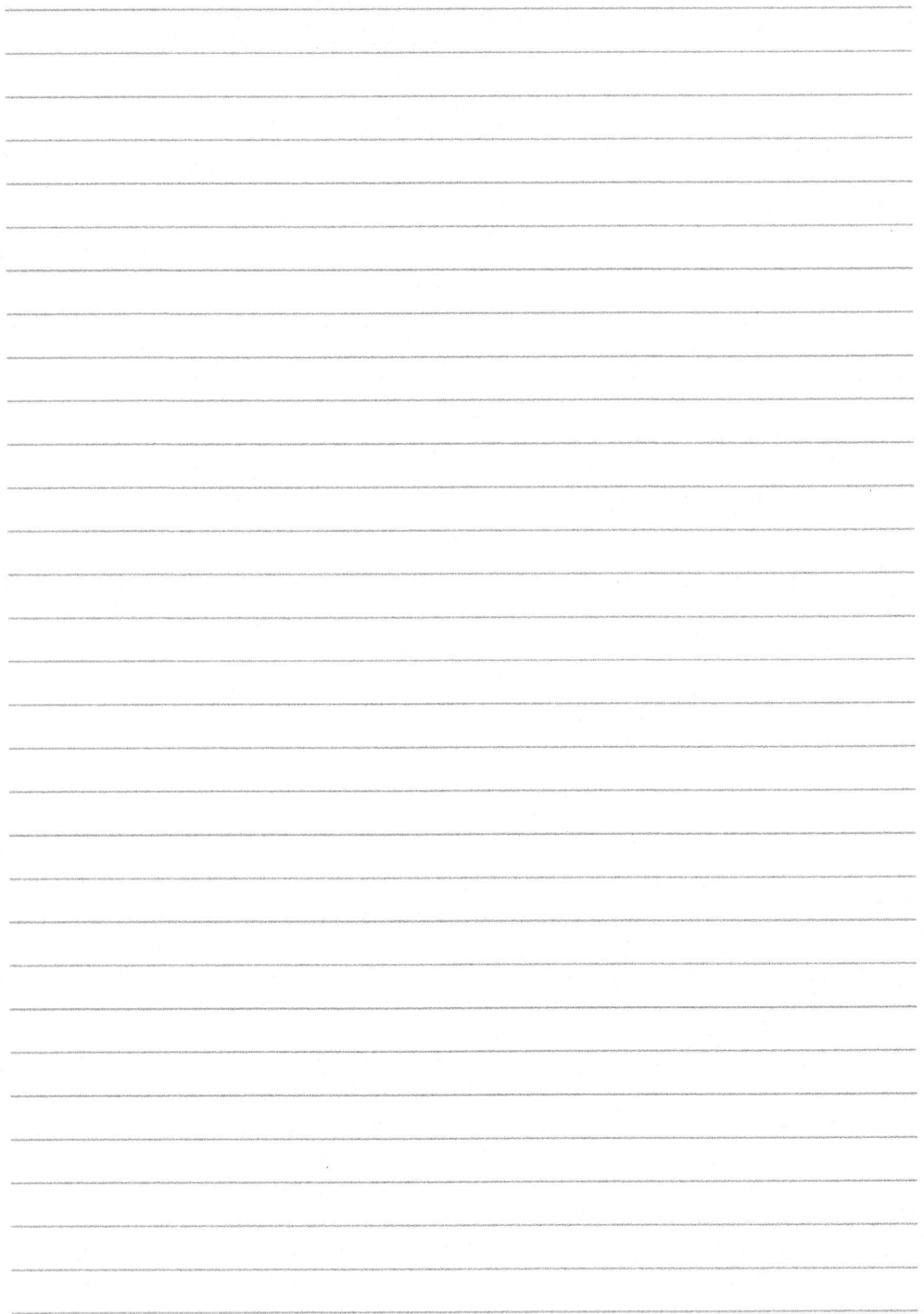

"Motherhood is the greatest and noblest of all callings." -L. Tom Perry

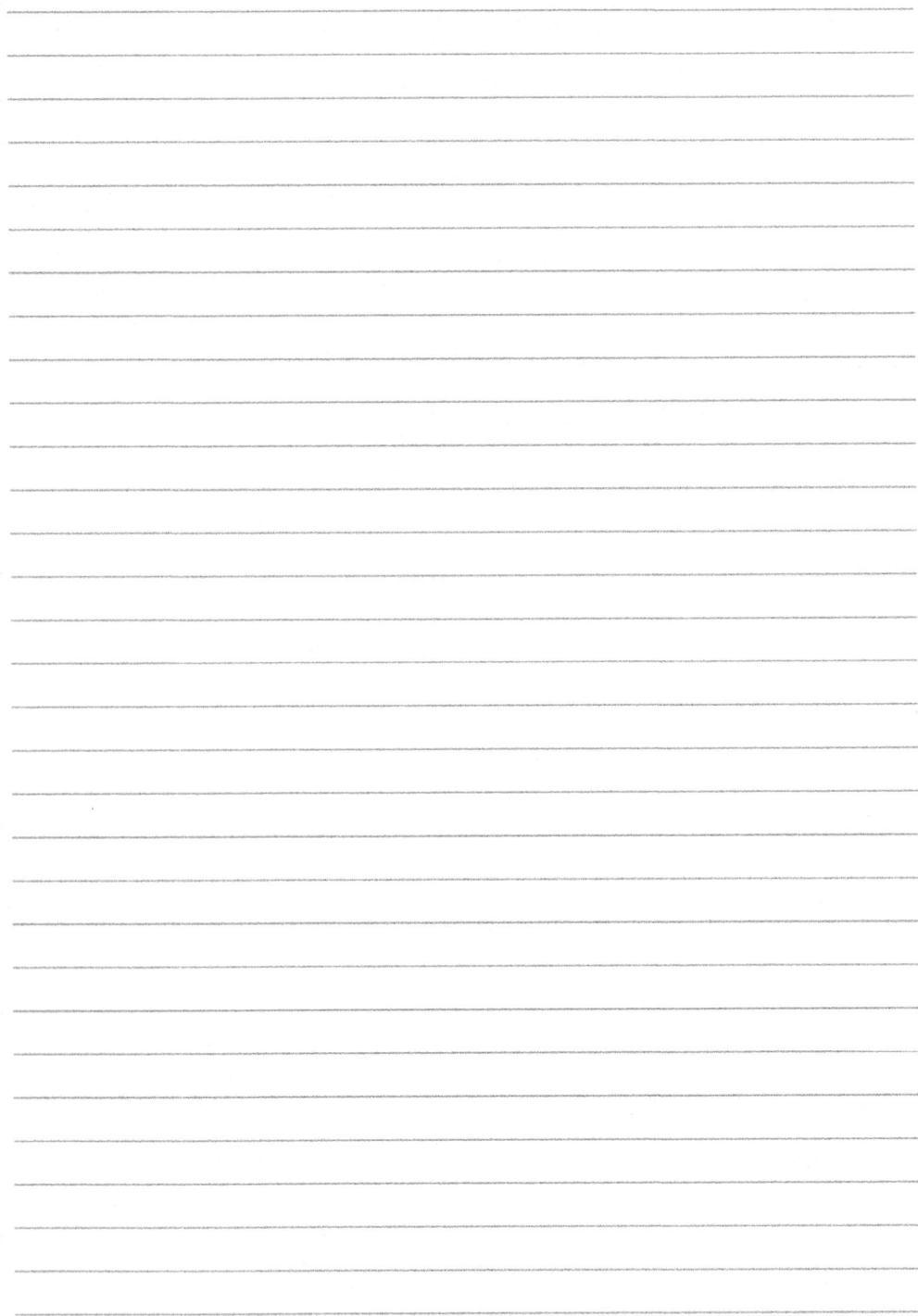

"I can imagine no heroism greater than motherhood." – Lance Conrad

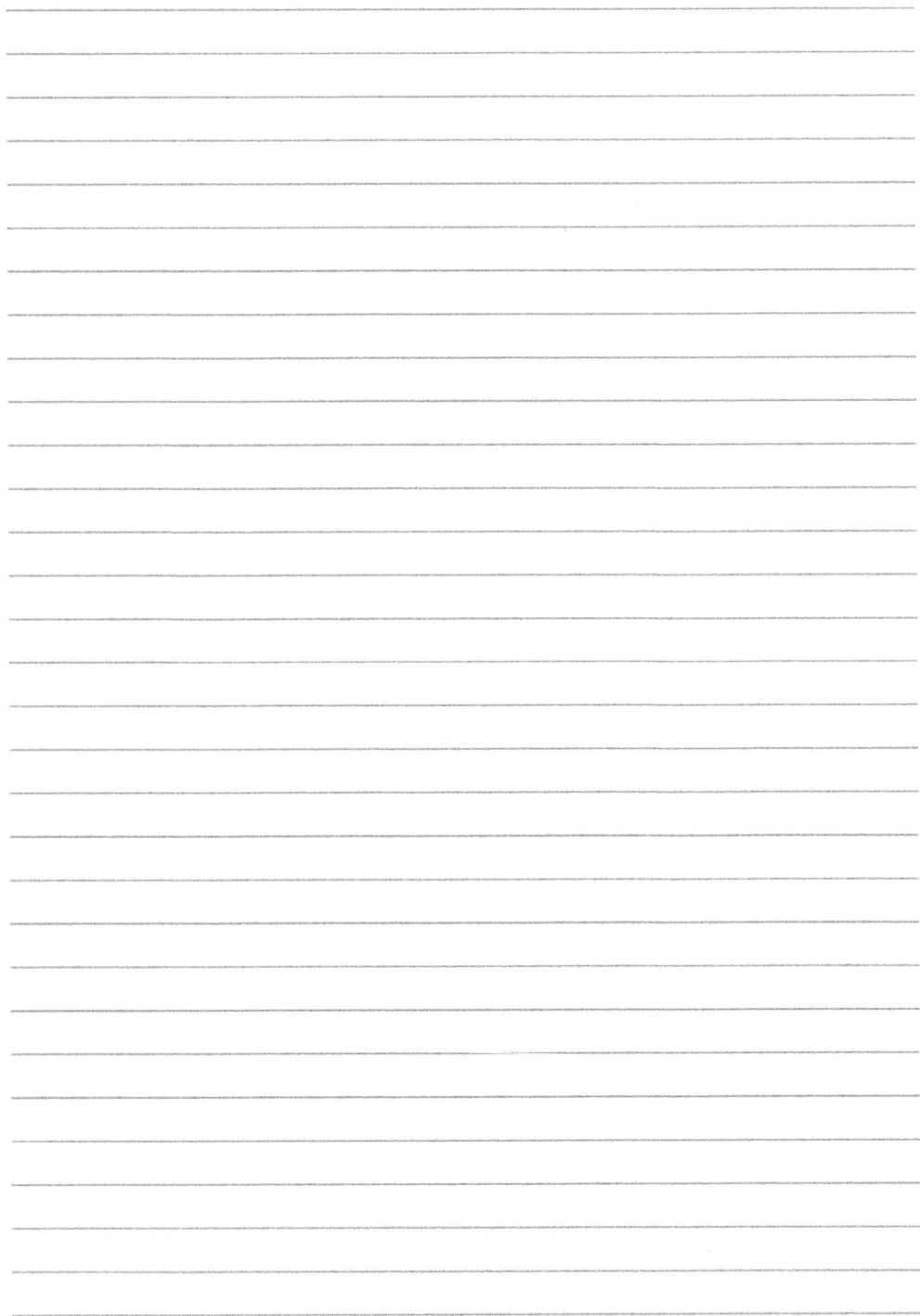

"Being a mother is an attitude, not a biological relation."
- Robert A. Heinlein

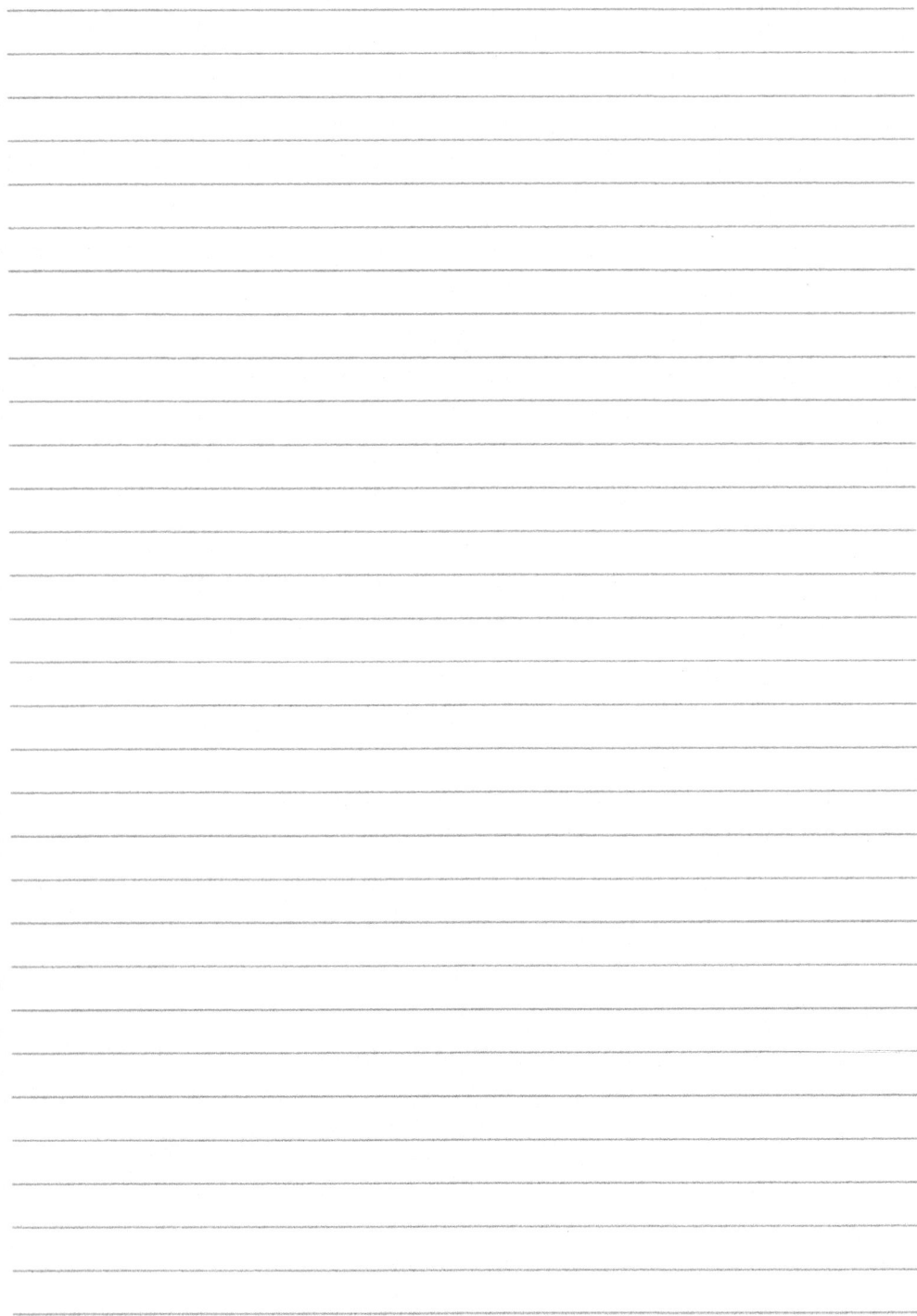

"Only mothers can think of the future because they give birth to it in their children.

– Maxim Gorky

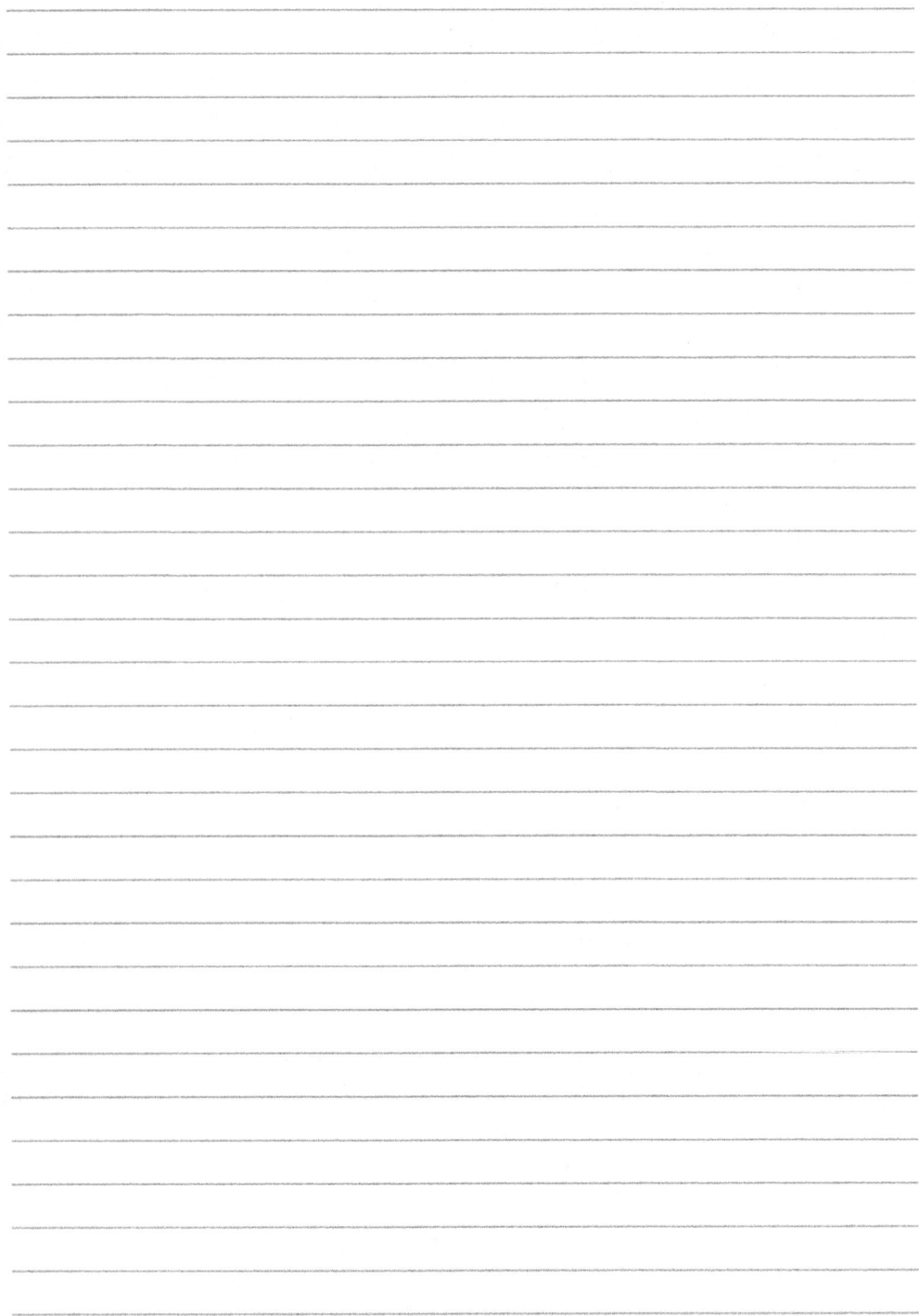

"Being a mother is learning about the strengths you didn't know you had and dealing with fears you didn't know existed." - Linda Wooten

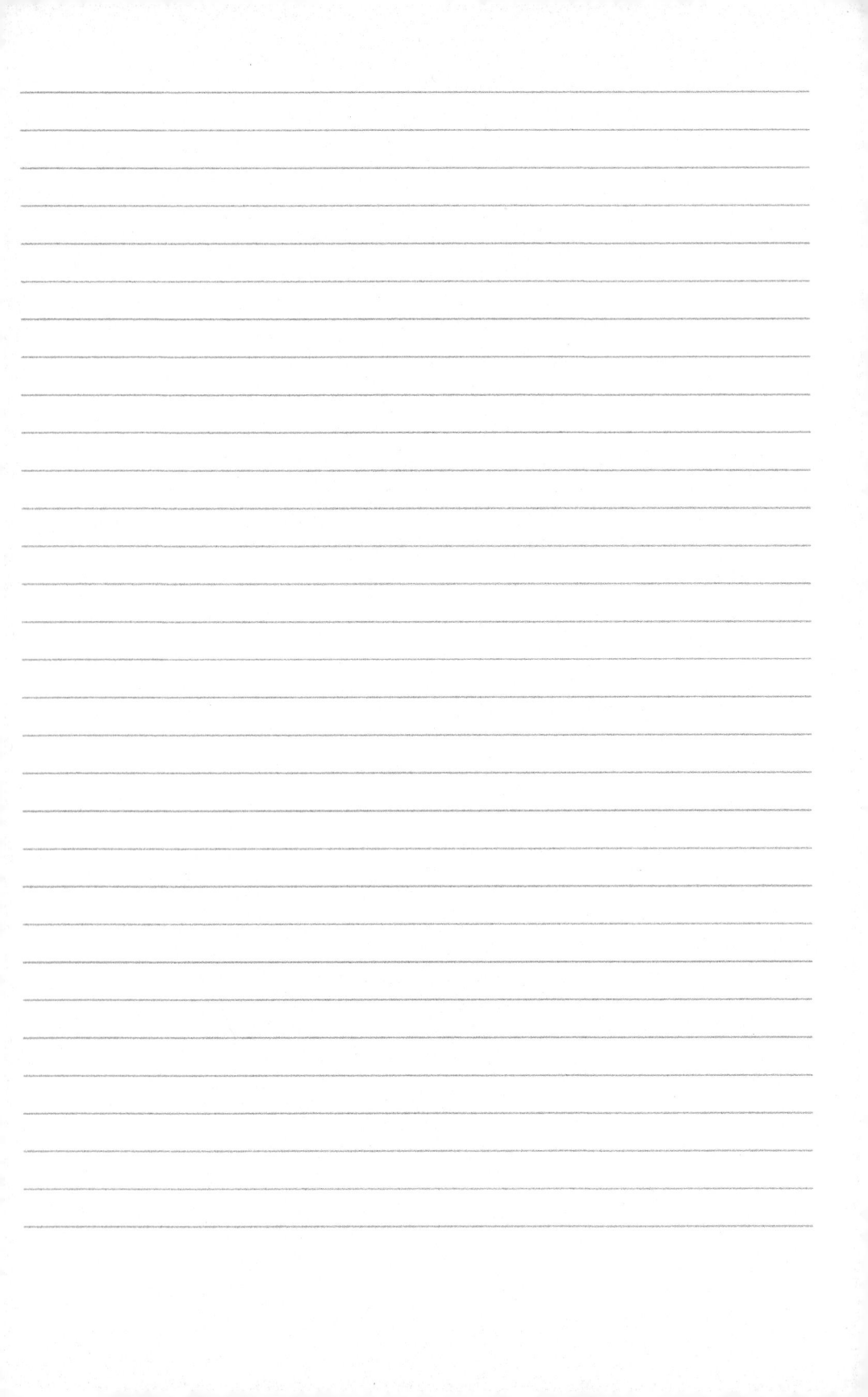

"Taking care of yourself is part of taking care of your kids." - Unknown

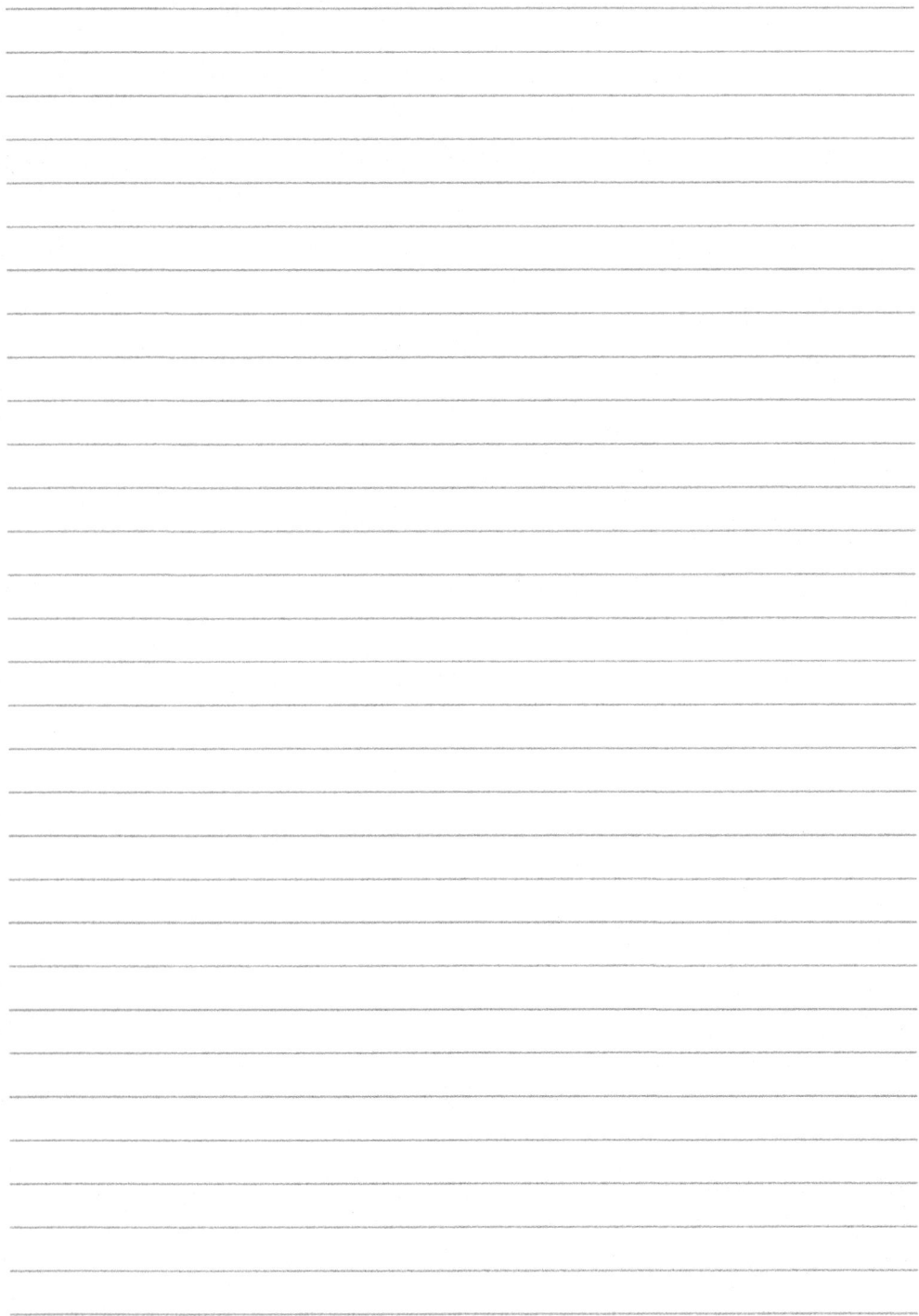

"To a child's ear, 'mother' is magic in any language." -Arlene Benedict

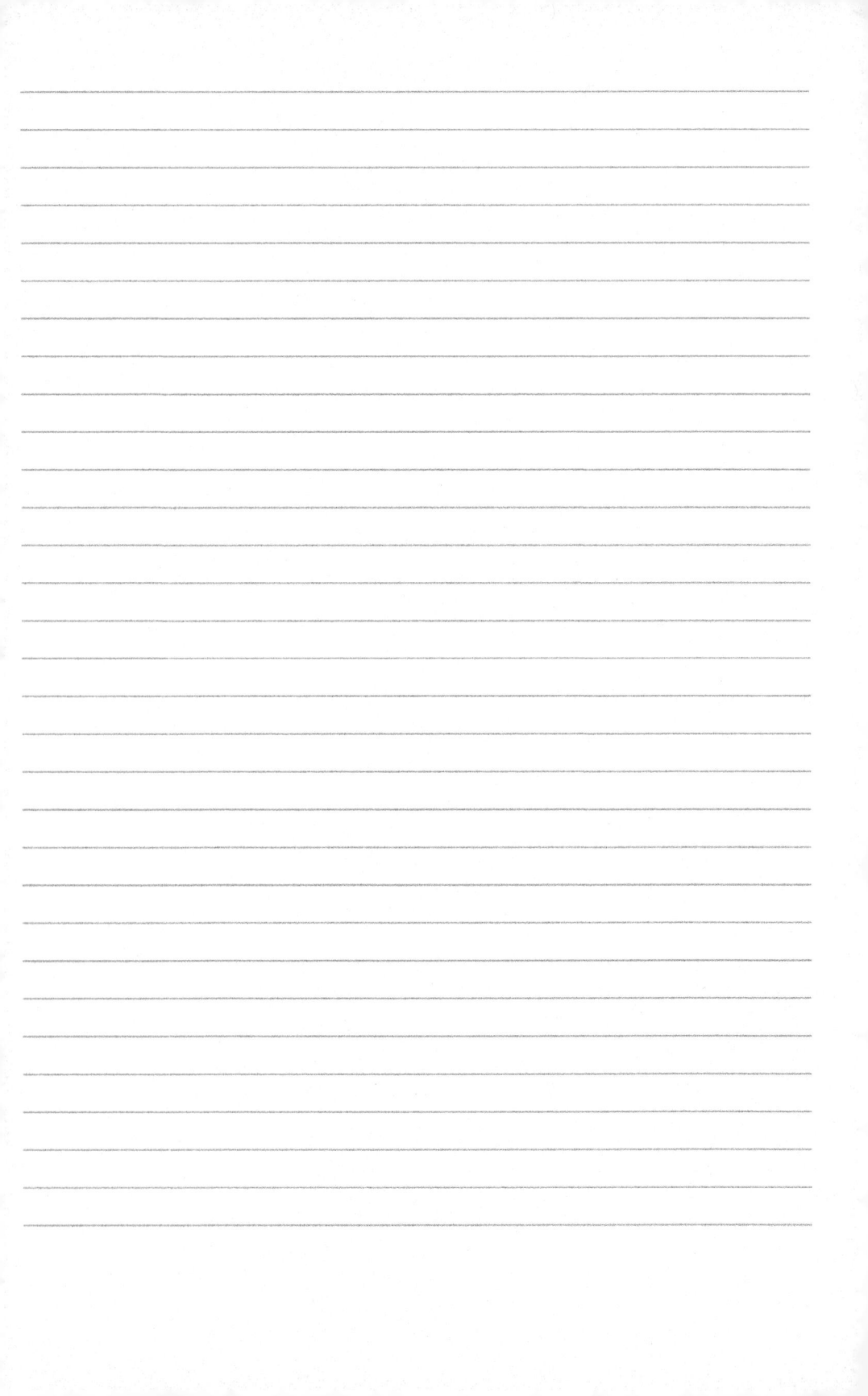

"Successful mothers are not the ones who have never struggled.
They are the ones who never give up, despite the struggles."
-Sharon Jaynes

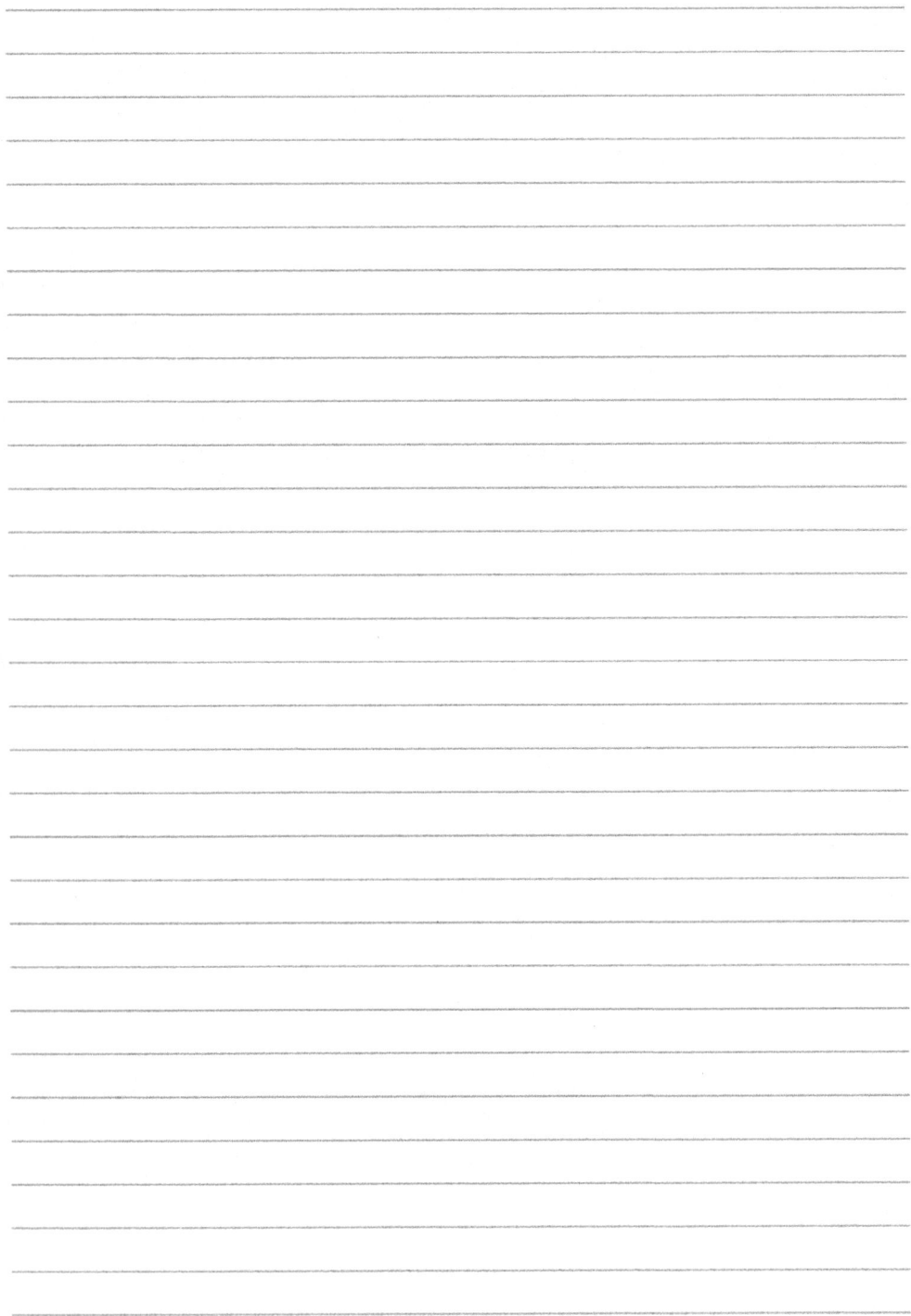

"I may not be perfect but when I look at my children, I know that I got something in my life right." - Unknown

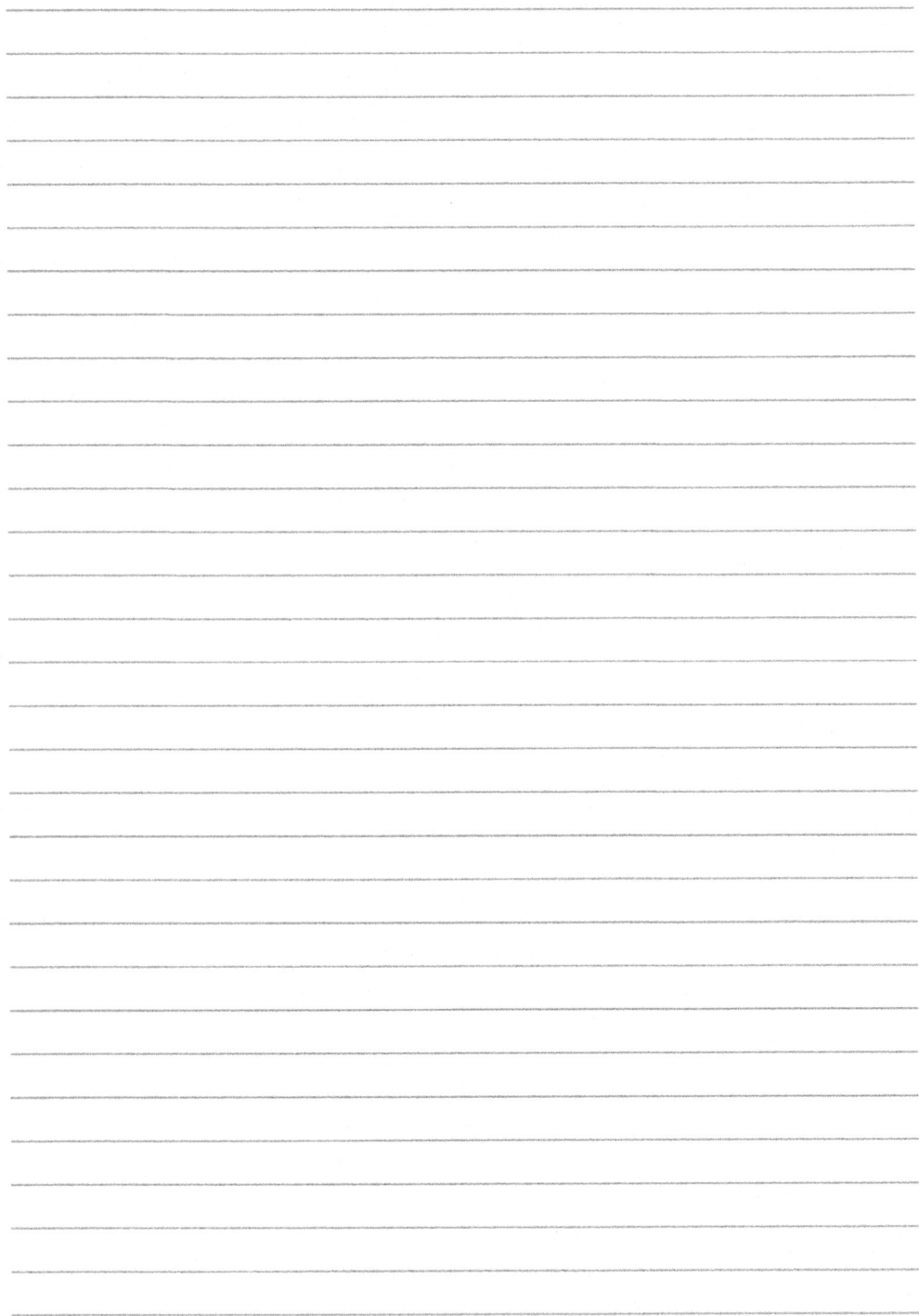

"Loving a child doesn't mean giving in to all his whims; to love him is to bring out the best in him, to teach him to love what is difficult."
– Nadia Boulanger

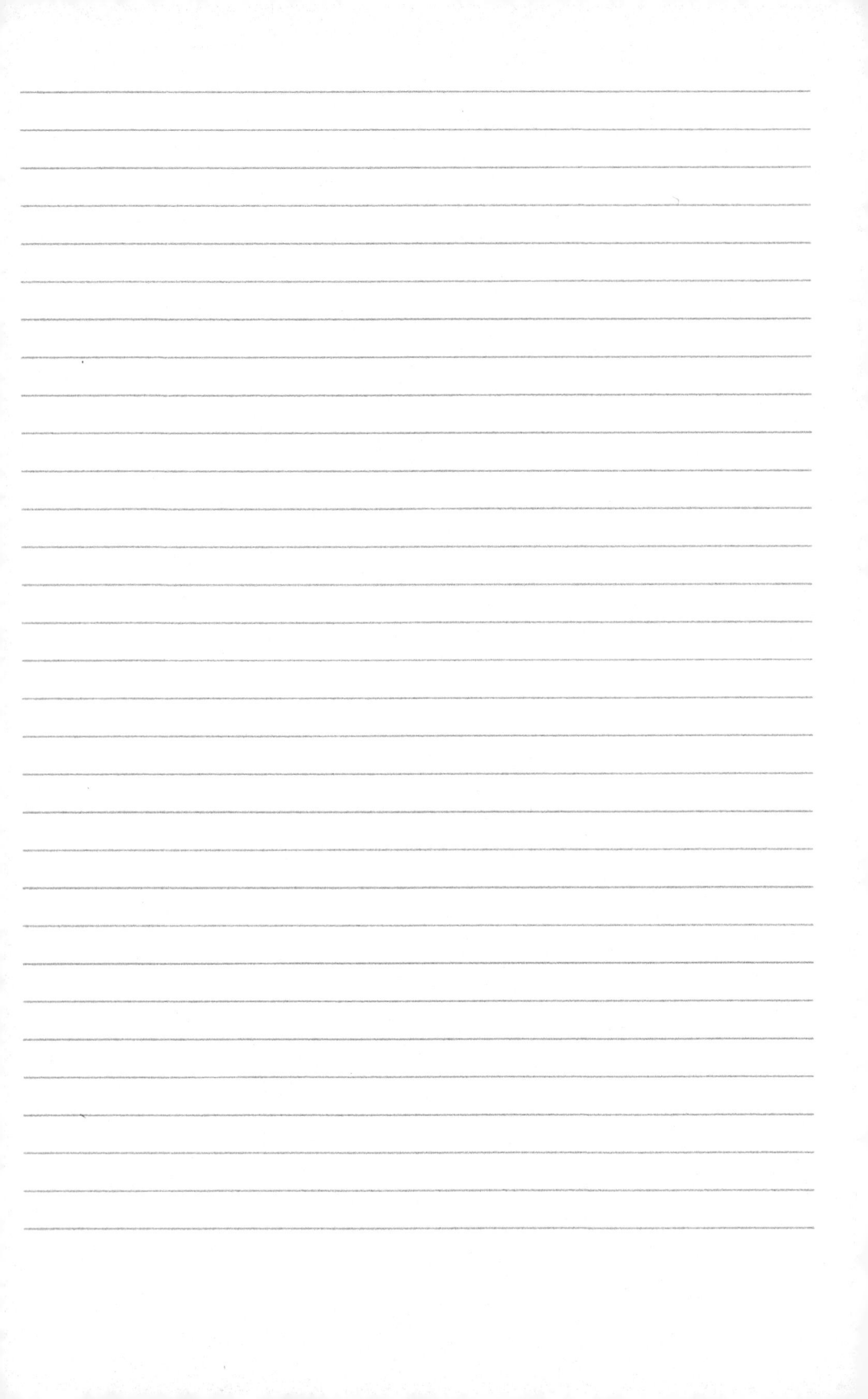

"It is time for parents to teach young people early on that in diversity there is beauty and there is strength." - Maya Angelou

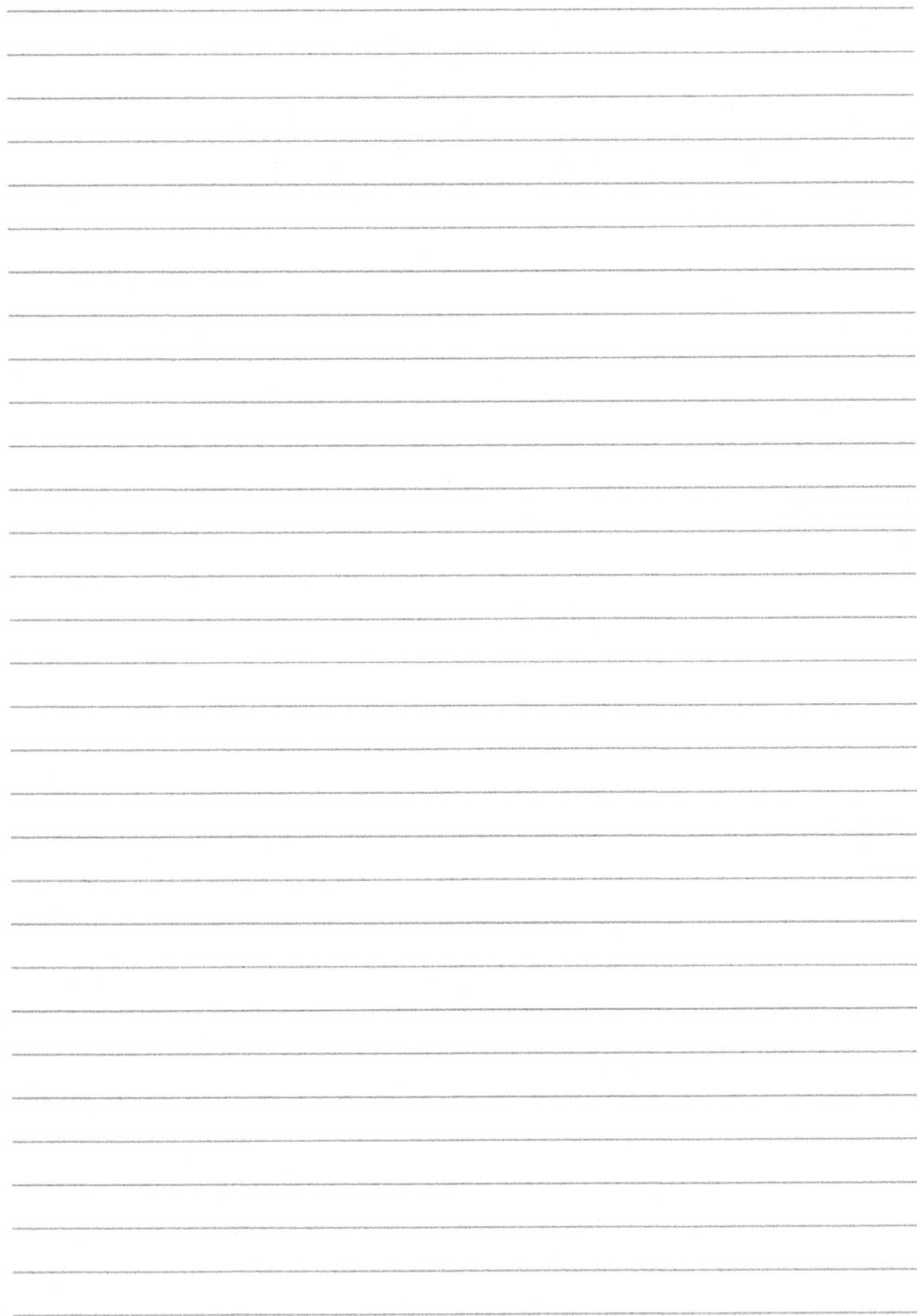

"The greatest legacy we can leave our children is happy memories."
- Og Mandino

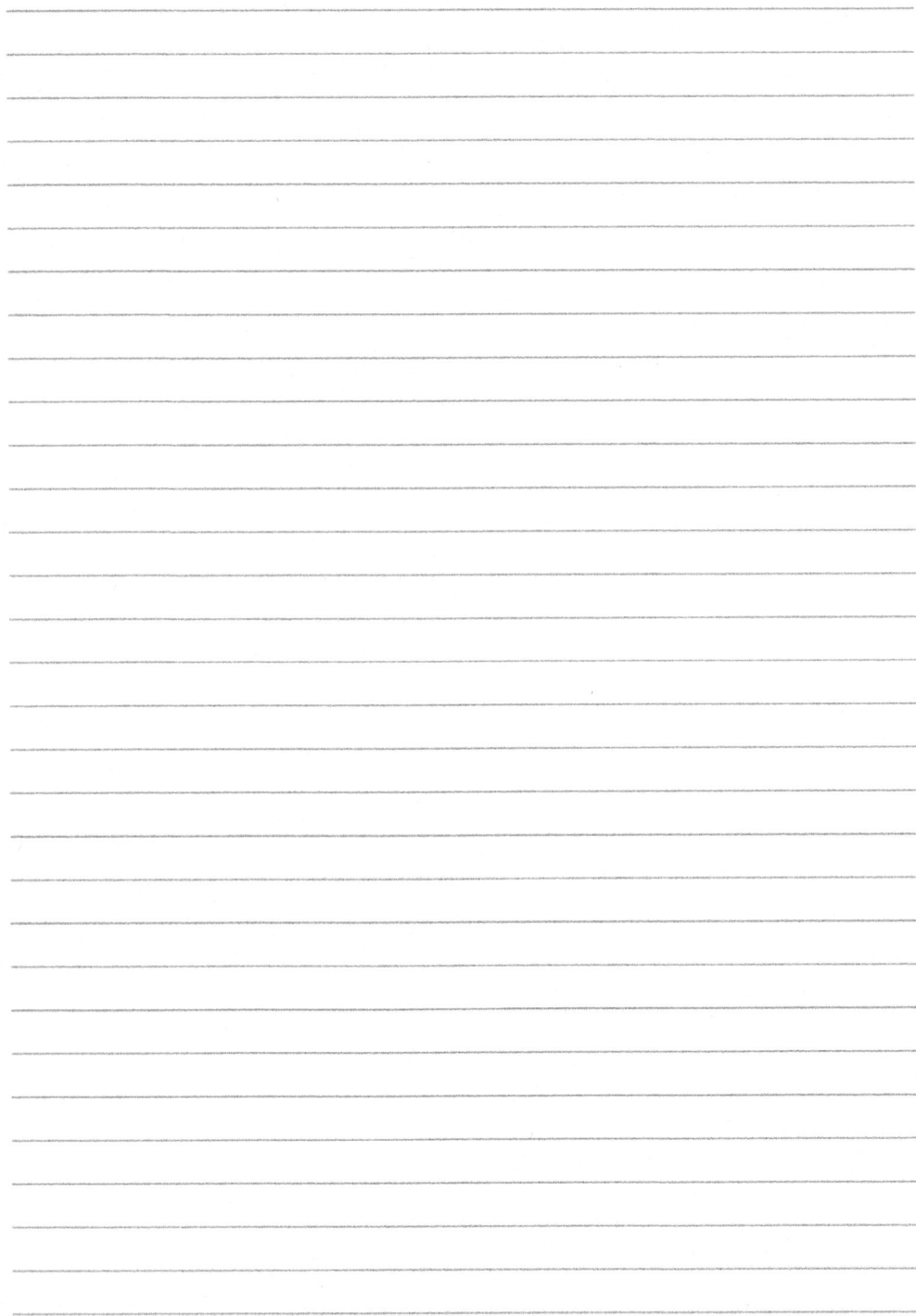

"If I have to choose between breathing and loving my children, I would use my last breath to tell them "I love you." – Unknown

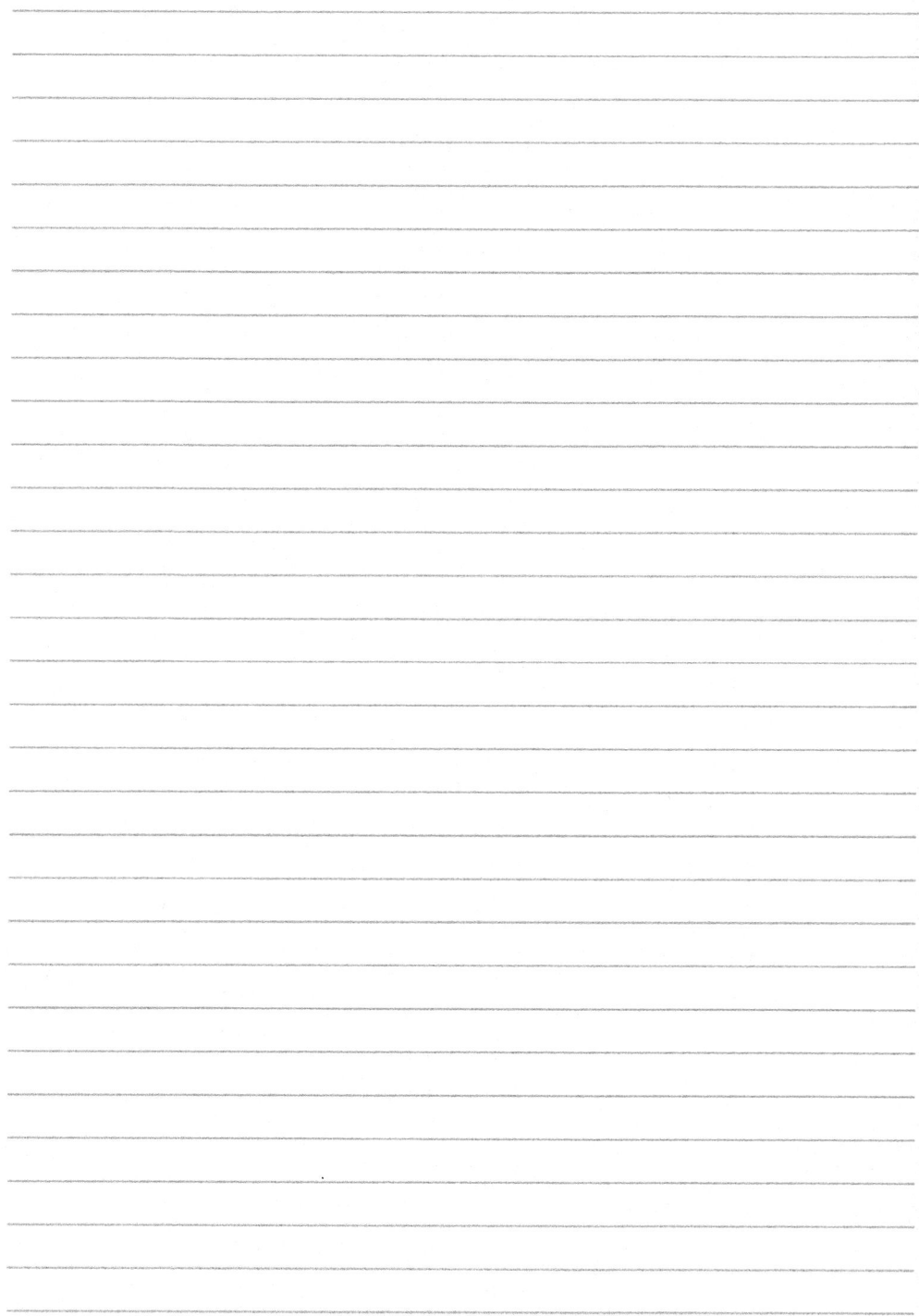